A DVD-based ~~Study Series~~
Study Guide

C. S. LEWIS: RELUCTANT DISCIPLE

Faith, Reason, and the Power of the Gospel

Narrated by Os Guinness

A DVD-based study series
Study Guide

C. S. LEWIS: RELUCTANT DISCIPLE

Faith, Reason, and the Power of the Gospel

Narrated by Os Guinness

Eight Lessons for Group Exploration

DISCOVERY HOUSE

PUBLISHERS®

Feeding the Soul with the Word of God

**The Daylight Bible Studies are based on programs produced by
Day of Discovery, a Bible-teaching TV series of this ministry.**

© 2014 by Discovery House Publishers

Discovery House Publishers is affiliated with Our Daily Bread Ministries,
Grand Rapids, Michigan.

Requests for permission to quote from this book should be directed to:
Permissions Department
Discovery House Publishers
P.O. Box 3566
Grand Rapids, MI 49501
Or contact us by e-mail at permissionsdept@dhp.org

All Scripture quotations, unless otherwise indicated, are taken from the
HOLY BIBLE, NEW INTERNATIONAL VERSION®, NIV®
Copyright © 1973, 1978, 1984 by Biblica, Inc. ™
Used by permission of Zondervan.
All rights reserved worldwide.
www.zondervan.com

Study questions by Andrew Sloan
Interior design by Sherri L. Hoffman
Cover design by Jeremy Culp
Cover photo: © fotolia.com/enrico113

ISBN: 978-1-62707-059-1

Printed in the United States of America
First Printing 2014

CONTENTS

Not Perfect, But Fascinating

Too often, we expect any prospective heroes of the faith to be perfect—or at least to reflect our view of how to live the Christian life. And if they don't mirror our personal standards or our interpretation of each facet of the faith, we sometimes shoo them off as not worth listening to.

If we were to take that tack in regard to C. S. Lewis, there might be reason to toss his literary works aside. Lewis was not a perfect man. He did things that some believers would say are not "Christian," or are not acceptable according to their reading of God's Word.

Yet in a sense it is Lewis' inclination toward imperfection that makes his writing so profoundly important. Lewis understood clearly the freedom and the forgiveness that we as mortals need in Christ's gift of salvation. Like Paul, who called himself the worst of sinners, or like Chuck Colson, who was a convicted felon, sometimes it is the imperfect among us who can best explain the necessity of the sacrifice of the only perfect Man, Jesus.

God equipped C. S. Lewis with a lifetime of experiences to accompany his remarkable ability to write clearly and succinctly—which all combined to enable him to pen some of the most well-loved literature of the twentieth century.

Lewis' writing was not limited to one or two genres, as is the case with many of even the best writers. He was able to write fascinating fiction that is loved by both young and old. He had the ability to write apologetics that have influenced many people to turn to Christ. He had the insight to examine his own losses in life and explain them in a great work about personal tragedy. Lewis' wide range of subjects sets him apart as a true man of letters.

In *C. S. Lewis: Reluctant Disciple*, you'll get the opportunity to walk with fellow Brit Os Guinness through the ups and downs of the life of Jack Lewis, as he was called throughout his life. You'll see the influences that colored his thinking, and you'll see him (as legend has it that Oliver Crom-well once said about his own portraiture), "warts and all."

You'll be fascinated by his relationship with his mother, who died when Jack was nine; his father, who never seemed to be especially warm to his two sons; and his wife, Joy, who didn't enter Lewis' life until his later years. You'll see how Lewis' writing was influenced by such varied elements as the landscape of Great Britain; his connection with J. R. R. Tolkein; and his faith, which followed a period of atheism.

Indeed, C. S. Lewis—who though like the rest of us was not perfect—was a fascinating giant of the faith. If you've read any of his works—and who hasn't—you'll be intrigued and challenged by this close-up look at *C. S. Lewis: Reluctant Disciple*.

—Dave Branon
Editor

SESSION 1

It Began with the Land

DAYLIGHT PREVIEW

Growing Up in Narnia

What is it in a writer's life that supplies for him the raw materials out of which is forged his work? Many who study C. S. Lewis are convinced that the beautiful countryside of Ireland made such an impact on his life that it became, in a sense, the land of Narnia in Lewis' magnificent Chronicles books. But it was not just the landscape of his youth that influenced the man who chose to be called "Jack." It was also Jack Lewis' family life that affected how he thought in his later years. When his warm, contented boyhood was altered forever with his mother's death when he was nine—and subsequently when his father sent him out of the country for boarding school—Narnia was replaced by a darker, much more serious reality.

—————COME TOGETHER—————
Icebreaker Questions

1. What is the most "enchanted" place you have ever visited?

2. How much did you like to read when you were young? What books hold a special place in your memory?

3. Did you have a nickname when you were younger? If so, who gave it to you?

 FINDING DAYLIGHT

Experience the Video

Feel free to jot down Video Notes as you watch the presentation hosted by Os Guinness. Use the space below for those notes.

───────────────── **VIDEO NOTES** ─────────────────

Geography of Ireland: Dr. Ronald Bresland

The Mountains of Mourne: Dr. John Gillespie

Lewis' beginnings

Father: Albert _solicitor_

Mother: Flora _degree in mathematics from U of Belfast_

Home life for Flora and family
Flora's father - rector

The mind of young "Jack"

did not like his name Clive

The move to Little Lea and Belfast (*Titanic*)

moved up in class
& Status

& built there
April 1912

Holywood Hills

just up from Little Lea

The "geography of Narnia"

Jack and Warnie's imaginary worlds

Albert's career

- Belfast lawyer
- saw money @ people as punishment

Flora's illness and death

Cancer - aug 23, 1908

Jack's life changed: "All settled happiness . . . disappeared."

Jack in England: Wynyard School

two weeks after mother's death

2 yrs @ School - school closed when headmaster declared insane

School holidays

Ewart family

substitute for mother's family

"A cheeky little brat"

what Ewart (first cousin of Flora) called him when asked later in life

WALKING IN THE DAYLIGHT

Discussion Time

─────────────── DISCOVER ───────────────

Discussion/Application Questions

1. Clive Staples Lewis didn't like the name his parents gave him. Can you relate to that at all?

2. Flora Lewis earned a university degree at a time when that was quite unusual. What effect do you suppose that eventually had on her sons?

3. John Gillespie recounts how Jack and his brother Warnie used to bicycle up into the hills in the summertime, where they had a tremendous vista of Northern Ireland. They could see north up to the Antrim hills, and they could see south down to the Mountains of Mourne.

   Gillespie states, "That sort of romantic sense of longing, that sense of feeling for joy, that sense of looking beyond, was starting even when Jack was really a young child. And there are those who say—and I think they're right—that the geography, or the topography, of Northern Ireland is part of the geography of Narnia."

   How does that background fit in with your memories and feelings of reading the works of C. S. Lewis, particularly *The Chronicles of Narnia*?

4. What signs did Jack show, even as a boy, of his creative genius?

5. Jack and Warnie looked forward to the school holidays and a month at the sea in Castlerock with their mother. Ronald Bresland observes that their father "viewed these visits to the seaside as sort of penitential, something that he had to do for the sake of the family. Albert Lewis was the breadwinner of the family, and that's how he viewed it. This whole Protestant work ethic, which was how Belfast was built at that time, was part of his mindset. The idea of taking a month off to lounge about on the beach was just totally alien to him; he couldn't consider it."

   a. How much does that value system remind you of your own parents?

b. How much does it remind you of yourself?

6. **What effect did Flora's death, and its aftermath, have on Jack?**

7. **A positive element for Jack and Warnie was the hospitality and care of their relatives, the Ewart family. Primrose Henderson's grandmother, mother, and aunt looked after Jack and filled in the gap after the loss of his mother. According to Primrose, they weren't always awfully fond of him, even referring to him as a "cheeky little brat."**

    How does it make you feel to know what became of that "cheeky little brat"? How can that provide hope and encouragement for you?

────────────────── BRINGING IT HOME ──────────────────

1. **What was the best thing about your own childhood? What was the worst thing?**

2. **How familiar are you with the writings of C. S. Lewis?**

3. How familiar are you with his personal life? What are you looking forward to in that regard?

DAYLIGHT ON PRAYER

Spending Time with God

1. How can the group pray for you as you begin this study?

2. Do you have any other prayer requests you'd like to share with the group?

DAYLIGHT AHEAD

Monumental changes are ahead for Jack Lewis as he continues his schooling in a land far from Ireland. Indeed, it is a spiritual decision to turn his back on God, the one he called "The Great Interferer," that colored his life during his next years. During these formative years of education and imagination, Lewis' relationship with his father was strained—yet Albert Lewis continued to support his son's education. He allowed Jack to move from a regular school to being tutored one-on-one by his father's former headmaster: William Kirkpatrick. According to one scholar, Kirkpatrick "strengthened the rationality" of Jack Lewis—a trait that would be so valuable once his writing career began to take shape.

"A Loss of Faith"

DAYLIGHT PREVIEW

"Not All Who Wander Are Lost"

During C. S. Lewis' high school and college years, he wandered. He wandered through the world of fantasy and myth in search of joy. He wandered from school to school to tutor in search of knowledge. And he wandered away from God in search of freedom from authority. Yet through his wanderings, he was never really lost. As Lewis' friend J. R. R. Tolkein later would write, "Not all who wander are lost." And one reason Jack Lewis' wanderings did not equal lostness was the reality mentioned by another friend, Walter Hooper: "God wouldn't leave him alone."

———————— COME TOGETHER ————————

Icebreaker Questions

1. What would you rather do when you were twelve years old: play sports or read?

2. What was your favorite sport then? Do you have fond memories of spending time in a library around that age?

3. In C. S. Lewis' early teen years, he became captivated by the music of Richard Wagner. What kind of music did you like at that age?

FINDING DAYLIGHT

Experience the Video

Feel free to jot down Video Notes as you watch the presentation hosted by Os Guinness. Use the space below for those notes.

──────────────── VIDEO NOTES ────────────────

Jack returns from Campbell College

Cherbourg School: Religious belief waned

"I ceased to be a Christian."

A search for joy

beyond happiness : pleasure

Jack and his father

went to this college on a scholarship

Jack at Malvern: athletics vs. scholarship

valued athletes over scholars

Jack had deformity of thumbs)

Private tutoring: William Kirkpatrick

pushed Lewis
questioned logic
started training in Presbyterian ministry

Jack considered himself an atheist

was confirmed to please his father

George MacDonald

Scottish scholar
touched Lewis' heart — holiness

"The scent of holiness"

he was attracted to scent of holiness

1916: Oxford

Jack's struggles with Christianity

equated it to ugly music, architecture

"God wouldn't leave him alone." — Walter Hooper

"Not all those who wander are lost." — J. R. R. Tolkien

WALKING IN THE DAYLIGHT

Discussion Time

────────────── DISCOVER ──────────────

Discussion/Application Questions

1. When Jack Lewis was nearly thirteen, he entered Cherbourg Preparatory School in Malvern, England. During that time, Jack experienced a loss of faith. As he put it, "I ceased to be a Christian."

    What do you suppose contributed to that process?

2. During these years, Jack occupied two worlds. In one, he worked hard at his studies while taking part in school activities. In the other, he escaped to a place of imagination and heroic tales.

    a. What do you think caused that dynamic?

    b. Have you gone through a similar process of escape, either as an adolescent or at another time?

3. Based on the video, how would you describe Jack's relationship with his father?

4. **When he was nearly fifteen, Jack enrolled in Malvern College.**

   a. Why did that seem to be a bad match for him?

   b. Looking back at your youth, can you relate to some of his negative experiences there?

5. **When Jack was nearly sixteen, his father concluded that he simply wasn't suited for any public school. Albert sent Jack to be privately tutored by his own former headmaster, William T. Kirkpatrick.**

   What effects, both good and perhaps bad, did Kirkpatrick have on Lewis?

6. **What impact did the writings of George MacDonald have on Lewis during this time?**

7. **Although C. S. Lewis didn't become a Christian until years later, Walter Hooper points out that "God wouldn't leave him alone."**

   How does that give you hope for your life or the life of others you care about? Do you have those in your life about whom you hope this is true—they have turned from God and you desperately want Him to capture their hearts?

Marjorie Lamp Mead notes that although C. S. Lewis had grown up in a Christian home, he had turned away. "He thought of God as the Great Interferer. He didn't want someone to tell him what to do, someone to order his life. He wanted freedom. And when he was able to convince himself that God didn't exist, there was just relief."

Lewis said of himself at this time, "Christianity was mainly associated for me with ugly architecture, ugly music, and bad poetry. But of course what mattered most of all was my deep-seated hatred of authority, my monstrous individualism, my lawlessness. No word in my vocabulary expressed deeper hatred than the word *interference*. But Christianity placed at the center what then seemed to me a transcendental Interferer."

1. Have you gone through a similar phase?

2. Is thinking of God as the Great Interferer an issue or obstacle in any way for you now? Do you know of a prodigal who uses this kind of excuse? What can you tell that person that might help him or her view God differently?

DAYLIGHT ON PRAYER

Spending Time with God

1. Given the encouragement that "God doesn't leave people alone," what person or situation would you like to lift up in prayer?

2. What other prayer requests do you have to share with the group?

3. As you pray, be encouraged by the words from J. R. R. Tolkien that Os Guinness quotes at the end of this session:

> All that is gold does not glitter,
> Not all those who wander are lost;
> The old that is strong does not wither,
> Deep roots are not reached by the frost.
> From the ashes a fire shall be woken,
> A light from the shadows shall spring;
> Renewed shall be blade that was broken,
> The crownless again shall be king.
>
> J. R. R. Tolkien, *The Fellowship of the Ring*

 ## DAYLIGHT AHEAD

The War to End All Wars ended the dreams of many young men in Britain. When World War I began, Jack Lewis joined up to help his adopted land's war effort. Unlike his friends Paddy Moore and Sergeant Ayres, Lewis survived the war to live out his dreams. In the process, he gained a new understanding of real life and real people beyond the fantasy of the books he so much enjoyed. His dreams continued on as he resumed his pursuit of an education at the universities, as he made his first forays into being a published writer, and as he cared for the mother of Paddy Moore.

Second Lieutenant Jack Lewis

DAYLIGHT PREVIEW

An Unlikely Warrior

While at the university, Jack Lewis had made it clear how much he disliked sports and all such extracurricular activity. Therefore, it would be hard to imagine him undergoing the rigors of basic training as a British soldier. But he did, and he was so successful in this manly activity that he worked his way up to the rank of Second Lieutenant. During World War I, Lewis lost at least two good friends in the battles, and he himself was wounded. As a result of his service during the war, he gained an understanding of people he would not have normally associated with, and he began a life-long friendship with the family of one of his fallen comrades. The war had a huge impact on this unlikely warrior.

——COME TOGETHER——

Icebreaker Questions

1. What is your favorite war movie? Why is it your favorite?

2. During World War I, C. S. Lewis experienced the camaraderie that comes with the battlefield. What is the closest you have come to experiencing that kind of camaraderie?

3. While convalescing after being wounded in battle, Lewis wrote his father and said he was homesick. Share about a time when you got homesick.

 ## FINDING DAYLIGHT

Experience the Video

Feel free to jot down Video Notes as you watch the presentation hosted by Os Guinness. Use the space below for those notes.

──────────── VIDEO NOTES ────────────

War interferes with Jack's education

Lewis volunteers for the army

Paddy Moore

Lewis as a soldier/officer

Wounded in battle; Warnie's response

Face to face with real life

The war marked him: "French Nocturne"

War's effect on the homeland

Jack's letter to his father

Publication of his poems

Paddy Moore's death and Jack's pledge

Back to Oxford; relationship with Mrs. Moore

Lewis deceives his father

A connection to Ireland

WALKING IN THE DAYLIGHT

Discussion Time

———————————— DISCOVER ————————————

Discussion/Application Questions

1. What kinds of thoughts and emotions do you suppose Jack Lewis had when half of University College had been converted to a hospital for wounded soldiers, he was one of only eight undergraduates in residence at Oxford, and he was exempt—as an Irishman—from being drafted into the British army?

2. Jack made a pact with Paddy that he would look after Paddy's mother if only Jack survived the war. What does this pact say about Jack Lewis?

3. What does the fact that Jack fulfilled that pledge by taking care of Paddy's mother—even deceiving his father to be able to do so—until she died more than thirty years later say about Jack?

4. What does John Gillespie mean when he says, "Depicting Lewis as an infantry lieutenant is a bit difficult"?

5. How do you think Lewis' experiences in the war negatively affected him?

6. What redeeming benefits came out of Jack's war experiences?

7. Have you gone through a situation or season of life that forced you, like Lewis, to grow up fast?

8. How did you feel as you listened to Os Guinness read the letter Jack wrote to his father while he was convalescing in London?

We know from the previous session that C. S. Lewis had a strained relationship with his father and resented him in many ways. In the letter Jack wrote to his father while he was convalescing in London, he said, "I know I have often been far from what I should in my relations to you."

After his father died, C. S. Lewis said that one of his major regrets was that he didn't treat his father better. Are there steps you need to take in regard to a particular relationship so you don't have similar regrets?

DAYLIGHT ON PRAYER

Spending Time with God

1. Based on what was just shared, pray for each other and your challenging relationships.

2. What concerns for yourself, others, or world events would you like the group to pray about?

DAYLIGHT AHEAD

It was no secret that Jack Lewis was a brilliant student. And once he finished his coursework with high honors, he moved on to become a professor. This new era in his life also included sadness, for Lewis' father died in 1929. It was another in a continuing line of losses for Lewis, leading eventually to his writing a book about grief. But for now, teaching captured his attention, while becoming colleagues with such greats as J. R. R. Tolkein would keep his sharp mind challenged intellectually and spiritually.

Sidecar Conversion

DAYLIGHT PREVIEW

"I've Become Awake"

As Jack Lewis finally moved from being a student to being a university professor, many changes came into his life. First, after Jack spent time helping his ailing father, Albert Lewis died. Second, as a new professor, Lewis became acquainted as a colleague with men such as J. R. R. Tolkein, the author of *The Lord of the Rings*. It was at this time in his life that Lewis, who had as a teen rejected God, viewing Him as the "Great Interferer," began to reevaluate matters of faith. And it was during this time that—during an outing with his brother aboard Warnie's motorcycle—he reawakened his relationship with Jesus Christ after a long period of dormancy.

COME TOGETHER

Icebreaker Questions

1. Jack Lewis received some remarkable honors as a student at Oxford. What high school or college achievement are you most proud of?

2. After paying for his son's education for fifteen years, Albert Lewis was relieved when he graduated. How can you relate?

3. As a young don at Oxford, C. S. Lewis enjoyed a daily stroll along Addison's Walk, a beautiful wooded path running alongside the college. Where is your favorite place to go for a walk?

FINDING DAYLIGHT

Experience the Video

Feel free to jot down Video Notes as you watch the presentation hosted by Os Guinness. Use the space below for those notes.

───────────────── VIDEO NOTES ─────────────────

First-class honors

Fellow at Oxford's Magdalen College

Albert's contribution to his son

Death of Albert: A door to the past had closed

Hugo Dyson and J. R. R. Tolkien

Lewis' first two poetic works and what they implied

"Convalescence from a long mental illness" — Warnie

"I wanted not to be interfered with." — Jack

Dyson, Tolkien, and Lewis

Riding Warnie's sidecar

"Valley of Humiliation"

Matthew 16:25–26

WALKING IN THE DAYLIGHT

Discussion Time

DISCOVER

Discussion/Application Questions

1. What emotions do you think Jack—and his father—felt when Jack graduated with remarkable honors from Oxford and then was chosen to become a member of Oxford's faculty?

2. Four years later Albert Lewis died. What effect do you suppose that had on Jack?

3. What does James Como mean when he says that although Lewis claimed to be an atheist, some of the poetry he wrote during this time was "some of the most compelling religious poetry you'll ever read"?

4. What did Jack's brother Warren mean when he said that he didn't believe Jack converted to Christianity, but rather it was like "a convalescence from a long mental illness"?

5. Michael Ward points out that Lewis converted to theism—becoming a believer in God—two years before he became a believer in Christ.

Can you relate to that two-stage process of conversion?

6. What role did fellow scholars Hugo Dyson and J. R. R. Tolkien play in Jack's turning to Christ?

7. A week after Jack's long and deep discussion with Hugo Dyson and J. R. R. Tolkien, he made a spiritual decision while he was being driven to Whipsnade Zoo in his brother's motorcycle sidecar. As Michael Ward recounts, Lewis set out for the zoo not believing that Jesus Christ is the Son of God. And when he reached the zoo, Lewis said, "I did believe that Jesus Christ is the Son of God."

What changes occurred in Jack's life as a result of his conversion?

8. Walter Hooper, however, points out that Lewis didn't go from being a formidable atheist to a formidable Christian right away. During this time Lewis wrote a few poems, but he realized that he would never be a great poet. "All the plans that he had made for himself were coming to nothing. He might not ever do anything *really* worthwhile."

Hooper believes that Lewis reached the Valley of Humiliation that John Bunyan wrote about in *Pilgrim's Progress*, where you have to give up everything and realize you don't really have anything to present before God. Lewis reached the place where he had nothing *except* God.

a. If someone of the intellect and stature of C. S. Lewis reached that place of humiliation, what is the lesson for the rest of us?

b. What do you take away from C. S. Lewis' journey in this chapter of his life?

──────────── BRINGING IT HOME ────────────

Walter Hooper says that during the period before C. S. Lewis committed himself to Christ, he was struggling like a fish in a net—looking for a chance of escape—because he knew that God would say, "You are now mine. You have to do what I tell you now."

How can you relate to that struggle?

 DAYLIGHT ON PRAYER

Spending Time with God

1. How can the group pray for you as you walk with Christ and submit to God?

2. What other prayer requests would you like to share with the group?

3. As you pray, give thanks for being able to discover the same somewhat painful truth that C. S. Lewis realized—in other words, that we have nothing *except* God.

   Jesus said, "Whoever desires to save his life will lose it, but whoever loses his life for My sake will find it. For what profit is it to a man if he gains the whole world, and loses his own soul?" — Matthew 16:25-26, NKJV

DAYLIGHT AHEAD

Something changed in C. S. Lewis on that day when he trusted Jesus Christ. Not only was he now redeemed spiritually, but also it seems that even his writing was born anew. And now, busy with a demanding tutorial schedule with his students at Oxford and his domestic commitments, Jack Lewis began to churn out the books that would inspire and fascinate readers for decades to come. But his works, at the outset, were not always accepted universally—especially among some of his university colleagues.

Writing: "The Thing He Was Called To Do"

DAYLIGHT PREVIEW

Writing and Speaking the Truth

When a transformed Jack Lewis began to put pen to paper with prose—having abandoned his efforts to become a great poet—the words were magical. Despite the misgivings of his Oxford colleagues, Lewis wrote for the common people. And the common people loved what he wrote. Once he had established himself as a writer, his fame grew when he was asked to address a troubled nation during World War II via live broadcasts on the British Broadcasting Company, the BBC. In the first decade and a half after becoming a professor, Lewis wrote such classics as *The Screwtape Letters* and *Mere Christianity* while becoming one of the most respected mass media voices in the land.

―――――――――― COME TOGETHER ――――――――――

Icebreaker Questions

1. C. S. Lewis loved to write. How do you feel about writing? Is it enjoyable or tedious for you?

2. Lewis enjoyed a game of croquet or badminton on the front lawn of his home. What memories does that stir up for you?

3. Lewis became well known for his BBC radio talks during World War II. When has listening to the radio been important to you?

FINDING DAYLIGHT

Experience the Video

Feel free to jot down Video Notes as you watch the presentation hosted by Os Guinness. Use the space below for those notes.

———————————————— **VIDEO NOTES** ————————————————

1931

A different man

"He crossed the divide." — Bishop Barrington-Ward

*gifts released when he
from poetry to prose*

Lewis' routine at Magdalen College

*7am tea
chapel
students   1:1
              1:2*

"Writing was the thing he was craving to do." — Walter Hooper

many put it off but I

Mixed reviews

*criticized as didn't have a
theological background*

Lewis' love of argument
didn't know his own strength in arguing
liked to win

Caring for students: Mary Shelly *— was as spiritual mentor to her.*
she was an atheist
free love
had an affair and was dumped
before her finals — then failed
Lewis encouraged her that she wasn't a
failure

The Kilns *— place where he lived*

Holy Trinity Church

The Screwtape Letters
written during Holy Communion
1941 as articles for Church of England

Lewis' broadcast talks on the BBC
during WW II
BBC demands exact timing which he needed
He was a communicator!

The end result: Mere Christianity
Compilation of the broadcast series

WALKING IN THE DAYLIGHT

Discussion Time

————————————— DISCOVER —————————————

Discussion/Application Questions

1. How did C. S. Lewis' conversion affect him as a writer?

2. What do you think Walter Hooper means when he says that writing was "liberation" for Lewis?

3. Who do you know whose gifts or creative imagination were profoundly released when they came to Christ?

4. What do you suppose motivated Lewis to write so many books and academic articles in addition to his demanding schedule at Oxford?

5. Many of Lewis' university colleagues criticized him for writing about religious matters when he had no theological training.

    How valid do you think their point was, particularly when Lewis first ventured into that genre?

6. Would you see Lewis' love for arguing as a weakness or as a strength in his life?

7. What can we learn about C. S. Lewis from the way he related to Mary Shelly, one of his students at Oxford?

8. Why do you think people who weren't churchgoers were so interested in Lewis' *Screwtape Letters*? Have you found them to be intriguing as well?

9. Why do you think the masses of England were so interested in Lewis' BBC broadcast talks during World War II?

C. S. Lewis was clearly called to teach and certainly to write.

    a.   What is your sense of God's calling?

    b.   How does fulfilling that calling give you a sense of liberation and release?

DAYLIGHT ON PRAYER

Spending Time with God

1. How can the group pray for you in regard to the discovery and utilization of your gifts and calling?

2. What other prayer requests do you have to share with the group?

DAYLIGHT AHEAD

Another new development in the life of C. S. Lewis occurred during the war when the British government sought to take children out of harm's way in beleaguered and embattled London and send them into the countryside to live. The Lewis household at the Kilns took in some of these children, which revealed the softer side of the great writer. At the same time, he and his writing friends, the Inklings, began to meet together to compare notes about their work.

"Transformed by Christ"

DAYLIGHT PREVIEW

The Man Behind the Books

As we look back across the decades since C. S. Lewis died in 1963 and as we examine the books he left as his legacy, it is hard to know what kind of man he truly was. But as we listen to what he did, what he said, and how he influenced those who knew him best, a clear picture develops. Jack Lewis, brilliant and talented as he was, appeared to have been a kind, gentle, fun-loving human who sought to improve the spirit of those around him. Whether he was taking in young evacuees during the war or entertaining older guests with his wit and humor, this man whose words were "transformed by Christ" and who became a world-famous author was above all a man who lived out his faith in Christ for all to see. Behind those books was a man of character and compassion and faith.

—————— COME TOGETHER ——————

Icebreaker Questions

1. When you were sixteen, who was your hero (or heroes)?

2. How much traveling by train have you done? What was the longest train trip you have ever taken?

3. What are your favorite memories of reading books out loud or listening to audio books?

FINDING DAYLIGHT

Experience the Video

Feel free to jot down Video Notes as you watch the presentation hosted by Os Guinness. Use the space below for those notes.

———————————— VIDEO NOTES ————————————

Evacuation of children

Jill Freud: Surprised to be staying at C. S. Lewis' house

"He was a hero."
never made her feel inferior

Life at The Kilns

The Inklings *group of christian friends → Joe Keen*

The writers read what they had been writing
honest critics

Father Walter Adams *~1940 - anglican priest*
↳ weekly confession

Sarah Tisdall: "He was enormous fun."
← "films don't portray the fun CS lewis was"

Lewis' goal: to please God through his life and his work

The prism of Christianity
write what God wants him to write.
wanted to try to explain Christianity
unless we find God we cannot
be what we are meant to be

Jill Freud: "He was a saint."
he was a good man
made sacrifices to be a christian

The metaphor of salt *compared to us*

WALKING IN THE DAYLIGHT

Discussion Time

———————————— DISCOVER ————————————

Discussion/Application Questions

1. Does it surprise you that C. S. Lewis became fond of the children who came to live at The Kilns during World War II? Why or why not?

2. What do we learn about Lewis from the way he related to Jill Freud, who didn't realize that "Jack Lewis" was actually the famous C. S. Lewis, and Ronnie, the young man who was mentally handicapped?

3. What do we learn about Lewis from his frequent weekend train journeys to military bases?

4. What do you think the Inklings meant to Lewis?

5. What do you think Father Walter Adams, Lewis' spiritual director, meant to him?

6. Assuming Sarah Tisdall is right, why do you suppose the films and plays about C. S. Lewis fail to portray how much fun he was?

7. What stood out to you about the spiritual foundation of Lewis' life in the last part of the video?

8. What aspect of that spiritual foundation do you wish was more representative of your own experience?

———————— BRINGING IT HOME ————————

C. S. Lewis found the discipline of weekly confession at first daunting, and then liberating. He wrote to a friend, "What a mercy to have another's voice to liberate me from all the endless labyrinths of the solitary conscience."

a. Have you ever been involved in a relationship like the one Lewis had with Father Walter Adams?

b. How could a relationship like that be beneficial in your life now?

DAYLIGHT ON PRAYER

Spending Time with God

1. How do you sense God speaking to you in light of this session? How can the group pray for you accordingly?

2. What other prayer requests would you like to share with the group?

3. As you pray, be encouraged by these words written by C. S. Lewis in *Mere Christianity*:

   "The more we get what we now call 'ourselves' out of the way and let Him take us over, the more truly we become ourselves. In that sense our real selves are all waiting for us in Him."

DAYLIGHT AHEAD

C. S. Lewis answered his own mail—and it seems that it came to him in bunches. But it was one particular letter, written by an American woman, that would bring huge changes to Lewis' life. In Session 7, you'll hear from Bel Kaufman, the author of *Up the Down Staircase*, as she describes this woman and the surprising relationship that developed between her and a man engulfed in a world very different from her own.

Joy and True Love

DAYLIGHT PREVIEW

Jack and an American Woman

As one listens to author Bel Kaufman (*Up the Down Staircase*) begin to describe Joy Davidman Gresham, it is easy to conclude: This woman could never be a C. S. Lewis love interest. Joy and Jack seemed to be so different from one another. But as Lewis himself was changing from one great university to another, so Gresham was changing from one worldview to another. An intellectual herself, once she became a Christian and began reading Lewis' work, she found a kindred spirit in the famous author. Eventually, of course, they were married—and another new phase in the life of Jack Lewis began. Their time together would be short, though, and Jack's "true love" died in the summer of 1960.

COME TOGETHER

Icebreaker Questions

1. In your household, whose job is it to go through the mail? How do you feel about that job?

2. C. S. Lewis immediately answered most letters he received. How long does it usually take you to answer a letter, an e-mail, or a text?

3. After nearly thirty years at Oxford University, Lewis made a surprising job change. What is the most surprising or drastic job change you or your spouse has made?

FINDING DAYLIGHT

Experience the Video

Feel free to jot down Video Notes as you watch the presentation hosted by Os Guinness. Use the space below for those notes.

───────────── VIDEO NOTES ─────────────

C. S. Lewis and correspondence

A letter from Joy Davidman Gresham

Author Bel Kaufman on Joy

    Bright and daring Hunter College girl

arrogant intellectually!

    Strange stages of belief

Communist → atheist
married William Gresham – rocky
marriage had two boys

Joy's conversion and friendship with Lewis

1952 - friendship

Lewis moves to Cambridge *from Oxford in 1954*
- offered a chair
new beginning

John Walsh: colleague at Cambridge

Francis Warner: student at Cambridge

Simon Barrington-Ward: chaplain at Cambridge

Psalms 86

The conditions at The Kilns
every weekend,
let house go to ruin
both brothers smoked
didn't bother

Joy and Jack: "Their minds met." — Bel Kaufman

walked every day at Cambridge

divorced Jewish woman

April of 1956: Civil marriage ceremony *@ Oxford*
legal means for Joy to
remain in England

Joy contracts cancer

March of 1957: Christian marriage ceremony in Joy's hospital room

↗ when it appeared she was dying

Bel Kaufman's visit to The Kilns

" Now they have it right "it" does exist
& love
Love — pure
— intellectual, spiritual

Cancer: remission, then return

July 13, 1960: Joy's death

WALKING IN THE DAYLIGHT

Discussion Time

——————— DISCOVER ———————

Discussion/Application Questions

1. What does it say about C. S. Lewis that he answered every letter he received?

2. How did Bel Kaufman describe her friend Joy Davidman Gresham, based on their days together at Hunter College?

3. When Joy later became a Christian, how can you see her being a good match for Jack Lewis?

4. After nearly thirty years at Oxford, Lewis made a surprising move to Cambridge.

   a. How do you think the faculty and staff at Oxford felt about that?

   b. How do you think the faculty and staff at Cambridge felt about that?

   c. How do you think Lewis himself felt about that?

5. What stood out to you from the recollections of three men who knew Lewis—John Walsh (a colleague at Cambridge), Francis Warner (a student at Cambridge), and Simon Barrington-Ward (a chaplain at Cambridge)?

6. What would have been attractive about Lewis' personality? What would have been intimidating?

7. Does the dilapidated condition of the Lewis brothers' house surprise you? Why or why not?

8. How would you describe the evolution of Jack and Joy's relationship? What role did their faith play in their relationship?

——————— BRINGING IT HOME ———————

Commenting on a translation of Psalm 36:1 that reads, "My heart showeth me the wickedness of the ungodly," Lewis said, "It does indeed. It does indeed. It's from my heart that I derive my understanding of that deep wickedness."

   a. How would that kind of self-understanding help to keep a brilliant person like C. S. Lewis humble?

   b. What keeps you humble?

DAYLIGHT ON PRAYER

Spending Time with God

1. How can the group pray for you and the concerns that are weighing on you today?

2. As you pray, ask the Lord to reveal to you the condition of your heart and how He would like to change it.

DAYLIGHT AHEAD

So what does one do with grief? Some mourn privately, partitioning them-selves off from a world that somehow moves on without the lost loved one. And some, like Lewis, share their grief with the world through their writing. After setting his thoughts down in his private journals, he opened up his pain to the rest of us in his classic *A Grief Observed*—for as he told one of his students: "the cure for everything is ink." In session 8, we get a brief glance at Lewis in sorrow as we enter his world of grieving his lost Joy.

Observing Grief

DAYLIGHT PREVIEW

The Gates of the City

And now it is Jack Lewis' time. Having ushered his dear wife Joy into heaven's glories, it would be just a little more than three years before he too would pass from this world. During that time he was able to publish his painfully honest look at sorrow and loss called *A Grief Observed*. In it the great apologist for the faith asked poignant and necessary questions that all who experience grief may either ask or wonder about. And then, too soon for this world, the light began to fade on C. S. Lewis' life itself. On one occasion, Lewis nearly died—"I've been up to the gates of the city," as he told a dear friend. And then, on a day that lives on as a hallmark of tragedy in America—November 22, 1963—this great British man of letters joined his Joy, and Jesus, in heaven.

COME TOGETHER
Icebreaker Questions

1. Are you more comfortable with small talk or with serious conversations?

2. Have you ever kept a journal or diary?

3. C. S. Lewis said he had no good photograph of his wife Joy, but her voice was still vivid in his memory. What person do you remember through either a photograph or his or her voice?

 ## FINDING DAYLIGHT

Experience the Video

Feel free to jot down Video Notes as you watch the presentation hosted by Os Guinness. Use the space below for those notes.

———————————— VIDEO NOTES ————————————

"He never showed any grief." — Francis Warner

expressed on page

"The cure for everything is ink." — C. S. Lewis

A Grief Observed *journal*
—N W Clerk - name replaced CS Lewis
most emotional book

Going through the valley
—in 1st three chapters
— parallel Book of Job

"A real man with a real heart" — Michael Ward

communication
c̄ emotion

Some resolution: Not pat answers, but a deeper peace

◊ end of the chapter

"To love at all is to be vulnerable." — C. S. Lewis

take risks c̄ love

Lewis' own medical problems

prostate, kidneys, heart
no pain

"He had been up to the gates of the city." — Simon Barrington-Ward

The day C. S. Lewis died: November 22, 1963

Same day as Kennedy shot

"Some day, God willing, we shall get in." — C. S. Lewis

WALKING IN THE DAYLIGHT

Discussion Time

--------------------------- DISCOVER ---------------------------

Discussion/Application Questions

1. Francis Warner recalls the time he went for his one-on-one session with C. S. Lewis and had the courage to ask the professor about his black tie. Lewis then asked Warner if he was married. When Warner replied yes, Lewis said, "You're a lucky man—my wife died last week. Now let's start."

    Would you consider Lewis' response unhealthy, or was he simply being true to himself?

2. Warner notes that Lewis used to say, "The cure for everything is ink."

    a. Does that seem legitimate or like a cop-out to you?

    b. Is it easier for you to convey your emotional state through writing—as C. S. Lewis did—or by talking to someone?

3. The diary that Lewis kept after Joy died became the book *A Grief Observed*. There Lewis wrote, "Where is God? Why is He so present a commander in our time of prosperity and so very absent a help in time of trouble?"

When have you asked questions like that?

4. Michael Ward points out that by the end of the fourth chapter of *A Grief Observed* Lewis is finding some resolution—not an easy resolution, not pat answers, not trite solutions, but a deeper peace. Lewis describes it as "a chuckle in the darkness." There is still darkness, but Lewis is now aware that someone is with him in the dark.

   How can you relate to that kind of resolution?

5. What valuable lessons can be learned from how Lewis dealt with his grief?

6. Those interviewed in the video make clear that Lewis came through the pain of Joy's death and then, in light of his own physical ailments, couldn't wait to enter the gates of the heavenly city. As Walter Hooper says, "If anyone was prepared—really looking forward, pawing the ground—to get to the Aslan's country, it was C. S. Lewis."

   What impresses you about that attitude toward death?

1. C. S. Lewis wrote, "To love at all is to be vulnerable. Love anything, and your heart will certainly be wrung and possibly be broken. If you want to make sure of keeping it intact, you must give it to no one and nothing, not even an animal. We should draw nearer to the love of God, not by attempting to avoid the sufferings inherent in any love, but by accepting them and offering them to Him."

   a. How vulnerable are you willing to be?

   b. What difficult situation do you need to accept and offer to God—and thereby draw nearer to His love?

2. What have you appreciated the most about this study and about this group?

DAYLIGHT ON PRAYER

Spending Time with God

1. How can the group pray for you in regard to your ongoing spiritual journey?

2. As you pray, thank God for His promises concerning what is ahead.

> For God so loved the world that He gave His only begotten Son, that whoever believes in Him should not perish but have everlasting life.
> — John 3:16, NKJV

> At present we are on the outside of the world, the wrong side of the door. We discern the freshness and purity of morning, but they do not make us fresh and pure. We cannot mingle with the splendours we see. But all the leaves of the New Testament are rustling with the rumour that it will not always be so. Some day, God willing, we shall get in.
> — C. S. Lewis, *The Weight of Glory*

> The term is over:
>   the holidays have begun.
> The dream is ended:
>   this is the morning.
> Come further up and further in!
>   — Aslan, *The Last Battle*